THE WAKING COMES LATE

THE WAKING
COMES LATE
STEVEN
HEIGHTON

ANANSI

Published in Canada in 2016 and in the USA in 2016 by House of Anansi Press Inc.
www.houseofanansi.com

20 19 18 17 16   1 2 3 4 5

Library and Archives Canada Cataloguing in Publication

Heighton, Steven, author
The waking comes late / Steven Heighton.

Poems.
Issued in print and electronic formats.
ISBN 978-1-4870-0094-3 (bound).—ISBN 978-1-4870-0093-6 (paperback).—
ISBN 978-1-4870-0095-0 (pdf)

I. Title.

PS8565.E451W34 2016   C811'.54   C2015-907258-1
                                               C2015-907259-X

Library of Congress Control Number: 2015955494

Book design: Alysia Shewchuk
Typesetting: Marijke Friesen

Canada Council   Conseil des Arts
for the Arts   du Canada

ONTARIO ARTS COUNCIL
CONSEIL DES ARTS DE L'ONTARIO
an Ontario government agency
un organisme du gouvernement de l'Ontario

We acknowledge for their financial support of our publishing program the Canada Council for the Arts, the Ontario Arts Council, and the Government of Canada through the Canada Book Fund.

Printed and bound in Canada

THE WAKING COMES LATE

CONTENTS

2   THE WAKING

For Eurithe, with more than gratitude

ONE

CAT SCAN

The basic subject of poets is their
own living body.
—Giórgos Seféris

THE LAST STURGEON

Deltawave shadows
of his deeds
and didn'ts, slid
under his shoes
like fillet knives, severing
soles from soil,
so he always walked
a little above his life,
not knowing it was
his life, while it waned
from waking-coma
to coma.
   Came a land-
locked night
he dreamed that he'd
landed the last sturgeon in the world
and she looked bad—
shrunken, bludgeoned,
a blue-ribbed CAT scan
of herself, her buckled
gills gawping,
a foam of green roe
welling from her mouth.

Each egg
was a tear, a tiny, entreating
vowel he couldn't quite hear
as he cast round the boat (now morphing
into a mountain shack)
for *water*, the merest

rainpool, he panicked,
or glacial stream,
my dearest,
my loved one,
let me bear you back
to haven—by river
the ocean
is never far.

INSPIRED BY A LINE BY PAUL CELAN

Betrink dich und nenn sie Paris

Each day I wake feeling I've already failed.
Tonight let's get wrecked and call it Venice.
A woman I loved lied that she was healed
and for a night until waking, we were. I was born
with a mortgage, now show me the house, the home,
slip me the dose that'll make me care less. I wake
each day feeling I've already torn
what I meant to rethread. (Did anything seem
in Eden, or was it all its own is?)

There was that woman, so enlisted in life,
one of passion's true recruits, *Love*, I said
I am so bad at loving, and the usual biz
ensued—scenes, loss and its isotopic
slow-fade, never done. On the deathbed of the skeptic,
where he slept each night of his dying life,
he said, *It was hard having so little skin-to-skin
with the world—but look on my works!*
                                        Venice
is sinking, and it might be the case
it was never the key at all. Said a small voice
in the cirrus of a dream, *Love is its own abode.*
Not sure what it meant, though I think I knew once.
There is some cold road that you must renounce.

I dreamed of cars
left for dead
with derelict combines
back of toolsheds
in bank-eaten
prairie towns

parked
god damn
down grave-
dark, un-
marked
lanes —

as if the writer who died
after decades unread
had stopped, and parked
where his map lapsed to margin,
carefully locked the car
and walked on

(pace these lines
bearing due west
in a foregone duel
with horizon)

no fuel
no friend
god damn
down ditch-
dark lanes

into autumn snow
into creatureless fields
no farm owns
no pen ploughs

LULLABY

Streu Ocker in meine Augen:
du lebst nicht
mehr drin
—Paul Celan

As for my eyes, you live in them longer, further
and still, sleep now and until, Love, sleep, slip away
into a cradle between waves

then revive, wake us both to these
stronger ensconcings.
Small wonder summer keeps returning

for you, more heat now but less
light in its supplies, happily bankrupt, volatile
August. As to my eyes, you move in them

deeper, somewhere towards, you sleep inside
the tendered words that serve now
as breath to both, serve also as bread,

though there's bread here too, so much to have,
the miser in the mind throws up his hands,
accepts a glass in sweet

succumbing. In these eyes you rest, for now
not mirrored merely, instead residing
in the lens of a briefly clearer

conception:
        live here less spectred
and fractured—held whole—sung back into substance
as I am by you, as sleep
                slips in, deeper still now, sleep.

VARIATIONS ON A CRANIAL CAT SCAN PROFILE AFTER A LARYNGEAL FRACTURE

Most intimate
of portraits, yet
clinically impersonal,

like a medschool textbook
graphic—cross-section
of a cadaver's

head and throat—or
a silhouette embossed
on a dime or quarter,

the chilling silver
of some undead realm.
You cannot love this monster—

the werewolf rictus
of grated teeth, the side-seen eye's
great, avid globe;

periscope esophagus, probing
up through the contused throat
as if to peer out

through the silenced mouth.
You might never speak again
in more than this rustle. So what

good now (wonders
the locked-in frontal lobe)
is this lobe, encased

in its hyperbolic brow,
the bloated cartoon
thought bubble

of consciousness. What use
if it can't express, explain
itself naked (save to itself)

or in thin, cold cuneiform,
as on this page,
two or more bone-shores

from life? So now, in the husk
of the broken voice-box,
see it mass on the scan

with that swelling—a welling
abscess of all you failed
to say, and might not now,

and the pressure collects
until you long to lean
an ear next to the lips of this

ghoul onscreen—to midwife words
if they strain half-free—
I meant to tell you, I

thought I told you, I couldn't
quite, but open, stay, God
help you if,

even now, you won't bear
into being, on a breath,
something

more than mere—

AFTER THE CAT SCAN

Larynx shattered in a crash and the doctor
orders you to gag it: "Pen and pad, pal—write
what you need to say." So you bronchiate
goodbye to your wife and daughter
and pack for the cabin at Desert Lake,
mute's retreat now, where you'll nod from the dock
at dawn-drunk anglers (bass, trout, and walleye),
who deem your pantomime thoughtful, fish-friendly.
Bit lonely in lack of the dog, who so loves
to boat in beside you, lunge onto the dock
as you ship oars, then disappear for hours.
But without your clamor to collar her back . . .
Three a.m.—outside, naked, you re-inflame
your throat chiding woodchucks chewing the frame,
your "yells" like whispers of a Scorcese thug.
(A long lag before they deign to scatter.)
        It's like you're an ancient, dreaming you're defunct,
striving to holler home across the river
that lets no sound slip back, not to wife, daughter,
even the dog with her large-array ears
who's loyally listening, shores apart—
who'll be listening for your tone of praise
until the hour her last faculties fade
and she hears only, faintly, the boatman's oars
stroking toward her like a muted heart.

AFTERNOON WITH CIRCUS & CITADEL

(*Paul Celan*)

In Brest, by the flaming rings,
in the tent where the tiger sprang,
I heard you singing, End-of-Things,
I saw you standing, Mandelstam.

The sky hung over the haven,
the gulls over the harbour cranes.
What's finite sang and what's constant—
gunboat, *Baobob*'s your name.

I saluted the tricolour banner
with a Russian syllable—
things lost were lost no longer—
our heart, a citadel.

BAFFLED IN ASHDOD, BLIND IN GAZA

Eden Abergil: former Israel Defense Forces soldier who, in August 2010, posted photos of herself smiling beside bound and blindfolded Palestinian prisoners. She labelled her Facebook album, "The army . . . best time of my life."

Eden
Abergil,
Eden of Ashdod, you only did
what any young recruit might do—
what I might have done myself, a little scared, a little
stoned (on your own strength, Eden,
as if each beautiful bullet you packed
were a pill—designer hybrid
of Percocet and blow, to anneal you against all
that's frail and slow, that's bound,
beyond help)—
      And so these Facebook pics
and that bit of bad press (don't worry, Eden, the news—
save on Al Jazeera and in the tabloids of Tehran—
has already moved on).
      You don't get it. You protest. Your little shoot
killed no one! So then, why are the great Jews—
the poets and performers, the scientists, inventors,
philosophers, reformers—those truest
People of the Book—all weeping quietly
in their tombs: Paul Celan,
Hannah Arendt, almond-bitter Mandel-
stam, Marx and Einstein, all of them sad
insomniacs of the hinterlife, tallowing
hours away in the earth
to understand this "Facebook," as well as the smirk

this now-world wears: failed future that won't leave them to
    sleep,
not even the adamant suicides—Benjamin, Levi, Celan—
especially not the suicides.
        And you sit baffled in Ashdod, Eden,
wondering why nobody caught the joke;
meantime the army's marketing folks
Photoshop your face to a blur, but
        too late, you're famous! Your poses
pathogenic, spreading via tweets and texts, and sickening . . .
        sickening no one at all—we've all gone immune—all
but the hopeful dead, though of course
they're dead and can't die again
of our indignities.
        Eden,
Eden of ash, your grand-
parents were the Nazi War—Eden
of Ashdod, *der Tod*
is still in the story, the frontier
between millennia didn't keep it out,
the Human Future didn't phase it out,
now it's posted, grinning, on your wall.

Let every wall wail.

LENINGRAD

(Osip Mandelstam, 1930)

I returned to my city familiar as tears,
as my pulse, as boyhood's swollen glands.
So quickly drink down, now that you're here,
the cod liver oil of these riverside lamps

and recognize instantly December's brief day,
where egg yolk mingles with ominous tar.
Petersburg, I'm not yet ready to die!
My telephone numbers remain in your care;

Petersburg, I have an address list still
to help me track down the voices of the dead.
I live on a black staircase, and the bell

wrenched out with its veins hits me on the temple.
Rattling the door-chains as if they were shackles
I wait through the night for the cherished guests.

THE CITY

(*Konstantínos Kaváfis, 1910*)

You said, "I will go to another country, another shore,
find a distant city better than my own.
All I attempt here is destined to ruin
and my heart, like a corpse, lies buried.
How long will my mind here mark time, wearied,
decayed? Wherever I turn, wherever I gaze:
the black debris of my life in this place
where I killed so much time: years squandered and soured."

You will find no other country, no other shore—
the city will follow you. You will wander the same
streets and enclaves, aging, in these self-same
rooms fading slowly to pale. Your escape will end
every time in this place. Don't hope for some other land—
there's no ship out for you, no road away. As you've wasted
your life here, in this small corner, you've destroyed it
everywhere else in the world.

WHEAT TOWN BEER-LEAGUER, GOOD SNAPSHOT, NO BACKHAND

Sometimes gladly I would skate away
from the simian prattle in my prefrontal lobe,
the desolate sierra of Mandatory Reads,
the whole envious exercise of Public Lit.

Then I see myself with you in some wind-burned
wheat town, raising cheerfully unsupervised kids,
you known locally for Odyssean dogwalks along the cedar
   windbreaks,
through the poplared coulees, and me
playing third-line centre in a beer league—you in the bleachers
cheering wryly, me bleeding a little on the hashmarks
after conceding another collision to Weyburn's most
cruelly goateed defenceman.

And the compound stink of the arena—fabricated frost,
the popcorn stench of old hockey gloves—would flag
a curious liberty from the fakery
and fuckery of culture—its pretense that one is special, elect,
consecrated to a purer calling,
                        when after all love
is the one calling of that kind, whoever hears it
and wherever, Yorkton
or the Latin Quarter, Medicine Hat or Venice.

(My slender, gentle mother, dead now ten years,
maybe it is simpler after all, happiness, goodness—
maybe you and Papa would have been as happy
in Kenora, or Cochenour, and sometimes
so gladly I would skate away—)

A COSMOS

In the wake of a month-long crimson tide,
as if the blighted sea were bleeding out,
phosphorescent plankton lapped the coastline, so every night
the caps of the great combers, luminescing
green in black waters, under a sky-tide of stars,
drew crowds down to Tragos Beach.

Third night somebody went in, and the father
followed with his daughter, fifteen, fearless,
their hands clasped in the caving breakers
buckling and torquing them under
as if to rip her free, her grip
loosening, her body in the sea aglow, looping
isotopic trails as she fought the undertow
in terrified delight, shrieking, swept back
into childhood, yet outbound as well
toward a life to come.
                                        As they broke
surface—sequined against the dark
by countless quanta of light—she seemed no mere
constellation but a cosmos, and even he
with his landlocked heart was portalled back
to earlier joys, and seas, yet by the same swell
cast outward years beyond the coastal
shelf of the familial, to a solo
unmooring: all ties, all selves.

They waded back through blood-warm shallows
and up the beach, the tracks they left
aligned, aglow, and fading.

"¡EVITE QUE SUS NIÑOS ...!"

1
On the shrink-wrapped shoreline a mourner
sits shiva for the seas: lapis
and lapping the last
living coast
with cesium.
So this is what a prayer is for.

2
Too late, I guess,
we learn what to love.
By the time I fell in love
with the planet
                    (a man was sighing
in the hypnagogic reefs of a dream)
it was dying.

3
And this just in,
approximated

from a near-extinct
lexicon

in a time of lethal
beachings —

                    the blue whales

                    bellow

                    below

UNTITLED

(Paul Celan)

What was written caves in,
what was spoken, seagreen,
flames in the bays,

among the molten names
the porpoises race,

here, in the eternal nowhere,
in memory of the over-
knelling bells in — (but where?) —

who
in this
shadow-quarter
is gasping, who
from beneath it
shimmers up, shimmers up, shimmers up?

THALASSACIDE

After the 2095 tsunami

On the shrink-wrapped shoreline a madman
sits shiva for the seas, lapis
and lapping the last living coast
with strontium
            as a castaway hamlet floats
eastward over the dateline (the village
retains its form, its dirt lanes now
salt canals, small Shinto temple
a flagship).
            In the deeps a deeper
quiet accrues, a Permian anemia;
the insurgent seas, on the face of it
victorious, still have to hoist
the foam-white flags of breaking waves,
as ages beneath the sun's farthest scope
carbon sea-caves (those eerie
protozoan parks, where all this began)
turn tomb.
            On a shoreline ledged like the lip of a grave
a one-man clean-up crew broods—your son, a centenarian
in eras after you—mourner late to the wake
or reluctant sage who has just seen through
the last possible proof of God.

COLLISION

Away in the eyefar
nightrise over the sapwood, and one likes
under hooves the heatfeel after sun flees, heat stays on this
smooth to the hoof hardpan, part trail
part saltlick now as snowlast moults back
into the sapwood
to yard and rot
and one sees moonrise mounding
over a groundswell, but too soon and swifter
like never the moon one knows, no moon at all,
two moons fawned, both small, too hot, they
come with a growling and
hold one fast, so chafing for flight
but what, what, what, what
wondering—

and one can't move and can't although one
knows from backdays, eared and glimpsed
through sapwood budwood cracklewood bonewood
flashes of this same Wolfing
                              now upon one, still
stalls the hooves on the saltlick and the eyebright
creature squeals   afraid?—and one somehow
uphoofed in a bound not chosen high as if to flee with no
trying, no feeling, fallen   flankflat, fawnlike
eyes above in the eyefar closing small
with the world

and now from the stopped thing
comes what   its cub?   legged up on its hinds,
kneels low to touch, but in that awful
touch, no feel   no fear to feel
no at all—

In the frail, obituarial
late November light
Essie ponders Sylvia's passing

and the caucus of crows,
those inveterate hecklers
cracking wise in the firs
outside the window.

They, at least, are dressed
for the occasion.

Her heart's concussed.
All that she must ignore
she now ignores —
her failure (it's almost dusk)
to transcend pyjamas,
the mournful cordillera of bills
and Post-its on her desk,
her inbox abscessed
with emails marked *urgent*,
though they aren't,
not this way — today
all is trivia, except for the sudden
absence of Sylvia.

Something's gone dead at the centre
and she stares,
now fully subtracted
from her outer life,

as these late,
low, oblivious flumes
of sunlight refill her wineglass
(and Sylvia's—still a kiss
of lipstick on the rim)
with a procession of shades—
    straw-yellow of Riesling,
        then amber Oloroso,
            then sweeter still and darker by degrees
as Sylvia's final sun unskies

but even this spectrum,
this memento she'd have noted
and savoured (like a spectral taste),
seems trivia, as everything
does and must and will,
save for the lone loss Essie
can't quite allow,
or swallow,

Sylvia.

She lays her cheek, slick with tears and snot,
on her mother's scarred and cooling chest, the breasts
years since removed, all flesh scraped bare
of the runged ribs beneath which now no stoic, solo
muscle knocks, and impossibly

a memory of milk returns—
the fleeting, timeless tenure of her suckling,
creamy sweet, yet salt as well, the feel
of life liquid in the mouth, now brimming
home to memory (if it be so),
                                    as her own milk
once swelled her own breasts, she awaiting
the nurse who'd bring her third child back,
the one they never brought back, so her breasts
seemed futile as the plastic sacs
hung here above a mother whose veins have ceased
to sip their saline,
                        each sac a clear
distended tear, the brine of her own tears
pooled on what remains of her mother's chest
as she—the child, returned—returns
that first life-gift of salt.

ARENOSA

In the cloud-forest
of her furthest mind—
quetzalled stands of tropical
pine, giant ficus, where thoughts
in guise of vines and
twining epiphytes subsist
on little more than mist, and insights
zipline above the canopy (its contours
like billows, rifts
in a giant green cortex)
                          I have been allowed
to walk at will, often
encountering the laconic
fauna of her odder
conceptions,
              the consecrations
of recurrent rain,

hours above the port towns
dense with diesel, beachfront
shills and pushers, chokered gringos
poached in chronocentric
fears (my fears), a few years
short of the bathos
of a first triple bypass—

Little one, so little comes near you—

In the cloud-forests her dreams preserve
step by step she walks her roots
deeper into sand, accepting
the tacit pact, blood-
mortgage in the marrow:
to die here, joy by
joy *I will* & loss
by loss
I will
        bare heels
impastoed with pinesap,
gentle largesse
of the duskfall dew.

SONG OF THE GRAVES

(J. E. Villalta)

  For years in the dry ledger of nights and days
their bodies barely figured. Now the debt,
in an hour, is amortized, a moment arrives
when the lovers no longer own themselves
or even remember how they met
or where, on the island
    of Arawak graves.

  The bone-boats of the buried dead, becalmed
in loam, are now less lonelied,
while you two, the newer ones,
lie here among them,
   relimb and become them,
on the island of Arawak bones.

  Nothing will ever be virtual again,
it seems—such spells
leave more to keep than this cooling
imprint of bodies in leaves (soon covered, hidden,
like time-lapse graves) on a shoreline's
border uncertained by reeds:
   a line between whatever loves
and what once,
     on the island of Arawak graves.

*Weather conditions current and overnight, temperature 9 °C
dropping after midnight to 3 °C. Chance of frost by dawn in low-
lying areas. Winds northwest 20 gusting 35 km/hr. Barometric
pressure 86 kilopascals and rising. Possibility of scattered flurries.*

The weather of other cities
signifies to new degrees whenever she's away — each day
you check and then check again
and wish you were there, or
wish you simply were
the wind, the cold, the snow that attends her — if in fact tonight
there's snow — or maybe the air
her face and chest will prow
at dawn as she steps out
onto Front or Shore. And searchlight spokes of morning sun
that fill her eyes you would like
to be as well, and so evoke
from the wells of each intended iris
hues not hers.
Has she layers enough? A polar front is pressing east
to frost the prairie stubble,
skeleton wheat towns
and ship-eating lakes,
and find her in Chicago, or Toronto,
by the lakeside, likely, her collar turned up (you turn her collar up)
and scarf tucked close
(you tuck her scarf in close,
and once again consult
the weather online, *Conditions
sunset, 6:08 p.m., unseasonally cold, skies clear, no moon*).

THE TURN

Everyone kept referring to "the turn
in the poem," and it troubled the poet—
she didn't understand. Perhaps, she thought,
in all her life's work there was no such "turn,"
nor in her life itself, which must then mean
her journey was simply a homestretch—
no epic detours, colourful car-wrecks,
no fork-in-the-road crisis where one lane
veered toward a fuller life, off-map.
                                    Well, tough.
Maybe her heart was always unmanic—
shy, but Shaker-steady. Maybe her poems,
like her mind, served more subtle metronomes—
so what? In her life no stirring, cinematic
turns, yet still her words make song enough.

Everyone kept talking about "the turn
in the poem," and it bothered the poet
that he couldn't see. Perhaps—the poet
thought—in his own work there was no such "turn,"
nor likewise in his life, which meant his road
was like a salt-flat dragstrip, he on it
pedal floored, no pensive pause, no quiet
fork in the forest of midlife—no sane
tap of the brakes and steering toward more
paced and patient tomorrows.
                    Glare off the salt
had long since seared his peripheral vision,
he saw only ahead, he went only there,
as on some grim, involuntary mission,
though his own poems, frantic, begged him Stop.

THE VINTNER'S LAST TASTE

I gave my life to the vine,
signed on long before you other fools
swarmed north with your schoolboy skills
to these frostbitten acres.

Growing, bottling, blending, tasting
and just plain drinking—all right, fine,
I drank too much! But God help the man
who outlives his vices.

Now the past year of my wasting
(cancer) winds down to this last carafe
shared with my wife,
now this last ounce, last taste of wine—

maybe the pears and cut grass
of a young Pinot Gris?
In truth I taste just echoes now,
but even so I drain my glass.

AN END

(Georg Trakl, c. 1914)

Over the white tarn
wild geese have fled.
Out of our stars at evening
this freezing wind.

Night's brow is bent,
broken, over our graves.
Under the oaks we sway
in a silver boat.

White walls of the city
knelling forever ... Brother,
under arches of thorn
we climb as clock-blind

hands toward midnight.

To give to the truth what belongs to the truth . . .
—Georg Trakl

The poet's grey hat, afloat on the lake, flags the place
where he marched himself under, his bowler
a buoy, last bubble on the waves
of the watery necropolis he might have dreamed up
the night before wading in—
gravefloats bobbing above the vertical dead,
a million floats, in files and rows,
over the weed-waving hair
of each head.
              Votive lilies and lacustral red
poppies flag where mourners oared past—mute
gondoliers with gifts—and on each float, epitaphic,
prescriptions in a stoned hand only Georg
(ex-druggist: now addict)
can grasp.
              From the shore, the others spy his hat!
Hollering they hurry down to restore him
from the green chloroform of the waters,
recruit him back to breathing,
enlist him back to life.

The war
the war
the war
has plans for Georg Trakl—
fate has filed fat dossiers of plans
for so many, soon
not even standing room

will remain in Middle Europe's
ancient lakes.

Now he coughs onto the sand
not blood but infant bile. *Smelling salts,
hot drinks: wake him back to this civilized dream.*

On the shore, a lipid spume like cream
on a field marshal's *Kaffee.*

And still the gentian current grieves
through the catacombs of Wolfgangsee.

CORONACH, POST-KANDAHAR

1

The damaged individual is invited to seek treatment,
albeit at some future date

Lance-corporal, here—
this comfort song, or (if prayer
is the protocol you prefer)
this prayer.

When you visit the clinic
we'll cook up a cure
for your sadness and panic.

Meanwhile pills,
meanwhile prayer.

Even to an atheist
God's the Omega
of a shotgun's business end.

2

The patient, still on a waiting list, suffers a major
coronary, for which he is promptly treated

His ribcage we cracked
and his heart we drew clear
like a red, writhing newborn
pulled from the rubble.

They said that in public
his punchlining brilliance
disguised desperation.

Take this, if you're manic—
come visit the clinic—
we've an opening
early next March.

Even to an atheist
God's the cold ordnance
of a twelve-gauge applied to the heart.

3

In which an appointment, of kinds, is finally found
for our patient

At the wake
(closed casket)

the piper
was drunk

but managed
a coronach.

MIKHALIÓS

(Kóstas Karyotákis, 1926)

Mikhaliós, they said, you're now a soldier.
Strutting, delighted, he set out with Vasílis
and Marís but he couldn't march, or shoulder
arms, or manage the simplest thing. "Master-
corporal," he was always murmuring, "Sir,
please let me go back to my village."

A year later, in hospital, he would stare
mutely through the window at the skies,
affixing a meek and nostalgic gaze
on some point beyond the horizon,
as if to find there someone to implore,
"Please, Sir, just let me go home."

But Mikhaliós died a soldier still.
His pallbearers were a handful of pals—
Marís, Vasílis, a few nameless others.
Above him they shovelled in the dirt,
though one bare foot they left sticking out—
poor boy, he was always a bit tall.

1

The Calvados by lamplight is an oily gold, a liquor pressed from bullion. Taste the essence of Norman summers—the fruit-sweetening sun, salt-bearing breezes of the English Channel, flotillas of cloud cooling the coastline. Proustian autumns, mellow and rich; the windless weeks of the apple harvest. Your snifter, brimming with brandy, exhales the scent of ancient orchards.

2

With your patient you are driving a dog-sled over a frozen sea under a sky trembling with a red aurora, blood pouring down a dark face. Your patient yells and whips the team onward. A bitch is whelping as she runs, dropping raw, mouse-sized pups onto the ice. The other dogs scoop them up and swallow them without breaking pace. You hurtle north toward that sky and, you are certain, open water.

3

The drink's mission is to italicize the effect of several dozen tranquillizers while masking their aftertaste. You arrange the Celestanox (7.5 mg) on the edge of your desk, in neat formation, like a cycle of birth control pills. This really ought to do it. You chase them with another full snifter and taste again those schoolboy summers at Grand-papa's orchard near St-Valentin.

4

The ones coming back from the war are the worst. You listen
and prescribe—rest cure, work cure, drugs. You'd rather not
prescribe them but you must. Even dust degrades to finer dust.
We find you slumped at your desk in a pool of your own fluids
and we revive you, pump your stomach, and your body survives.
Bodies are made to, minds not so much. The ones that come
back from the war, etcetera. Even dust falls to finer dust.

5

Your patient grew up in northern Quebec, son of a white
trapper and Inuit mother. At twenty, Pete saw the war as a
way out. And so it was. Up there everyone knew how to use a
shotgun, he said, because of the fucking bears, though he
never had to kill one. He did waste a guy in Panjwai with his
C7 and it wasn't like online. Wasn't even a man—wouldn't a
man over there have a beard?
  "Yes, I fear so."
  Doctor, feel but don't overfeel.

6

Above all, don't get too involved! You can care but you must
not love! Up north, when a big tide went out, they could crawl
and then walk under the ice and it was alcohol blue and they
could hear the sea in the far off and Sorels treading above.
Pete kept coming back to that, curled like a glove in his chair.
Many came home like him, but not all kept shotguns ready.
When the tide returns, man, you gotta move fast!
  Doctor, I order you not to love.

We killed with the best of intentions.
The goals that we died for were sound.
The notions we killed for were sterling,
our motives the sort that one mentions,
frankly, with pride.
                              Quit scrupling,
quibbling, lying down and
lay this down:
                    Bad guys by the graveful we gunned down so
                              girls, little girls
by the classful, could go to school. Girls, too, busing to school,
        we slew so girls could go to school unharmed, in error
we slew them, with better intentions, bad eggs however we *harmed*
              to win hearts, warm cockles, gain guts and livers and
                    limbs and minds
with decent intentions, good eggs we even armed (only good eggs
        armed)—the rest we smashed, truncated,
atomized until the doves among us
                                    buckled, seldom seeing dead
                                        men un-
        dismantled, while heads of this and that kept touting,
hawking our cause like crack,
        our crystal intentions, motives one mentions
especially when aim is less than exact
        and friendlies get fried . . .

With downsized intentions we killed and we strafed
and we mortared and missiled and mined,
sniped too, droned too,
        till we wilted to haunts in OSI wards, nightly

wading tarns and tar-ponds incarnadine,
and they dosed and discharged and forsook us,
but on we kept killing with credible reasons
in a lush neural loop of gibbering visions
from hovering gunships, maniacally hooting,
culling the groundlings with motives forgotten
to a playlist of metal eternally cycling . . .

Of course, looking back, you would like to reboot
and start over, but there is no over—
this spraying and shredding forever recursive—
this Gatling drum always ample with ammo—
and papa and papa our weapons keep bleating—
a ceaseless returning and endless rehearsing—
you're killing with the best of
with the best of them
killing with the best of
with the best of them, killing,

would like a word with you about the children.
Will he need a passport couriered from heaven
to cross the counterfeit borders of the Vatican
and reach your HQ?
                              I'd answer frankly, in your position.
You weren't expecting this, I realize.
Drone-high on cortisol, cocktailed, lionized
in the cloudhouse suites of Manhattan,
Bernie M. didn't expect the Inquisition
either. (He too had certain schemes
that took in the trusting—but maybe power
isn't impunity forever?)
I admit it's bad manners
to remark on the cries half-heard
from the cesspit of history's cellars
(at least in the moments we look up from our screens)
but—just for the hell of it—
I'll ask: how many profaned and punished
(as if they were the sinners!)
on your watch; how many celibate
molesters airlifted to Africa, where, I guess,
you guessed they'd do less damage,
at least to the Church, its whited image.
Why, even some of the faithful feel shaken,
half-wakened—half-hoping to hear Jesus
deliver a *j'accuse*
before your guards work him over in Roman
style, then bounce him,
a Jew, from your private club, renounce him,
keep your little statelet pure.

                    Father, I'm guessing
that button you're pressing
will bring the Swiss Guards.
                    So let me conclude:
of course I'm assuming
should it come to a trial
                    (though God
Himself bear witness)
                    you'd walk,
and your hacks would go on blaming
atheists like Hitch and Dawk
for smearing the See, while some loyal,
dispensable bishop takes the fall. *C'est la vie.*
But surely as CEO you'll need
to say something more about your brand—
or even come clean about the *lex naturae,*
that good Old Testament protocol?
Herzog put it best in *Aguirre,*
The Wrath of God:
the Church was always on the side of the strong.

LOT'S WIFE

(*Anna Akhmatova, 1924*)

But his wife looked back from behind him, and she became a pillar of salt.
—Genesis 19:26

The just man followed God's vast and shining
messenger over the black mountainside,
but in his wife a voice kept keening,
"It's still not too late—look back one more time

at the red towers of your native Sodom,
the square you sang in, the garden where you wove,
the high windows of that abandoned home
where you bore Lot the children of your love."

As she turned to look back, a scorching volt
of pain shot into her eyes—she was blind,
her body turning into transparent salt,
her swift legs taking root in the ground.

Who will weep for a lone woman like her,
one small loss in a history of grief?
Still, in my heart I can never forget her.
For a last look home, she gave up her life.

LOT LOOKED BACK FIRST

The "just man" never thought he'd disobey.
Yet even before she—a few steps ahead—
widowed him with a homeward glance, his eye
too grew restive, as if more afraid

not to look than to look: the high-walled home
he'd built her himself, the cedar-shuttered
window by the bed, his old dog—too lame,
disdaining a last bone—and the laddered

rooftop he'd climb to at dusk with his daughter.
But fearing loss (not just life but rank—Lot
as laurelled public man, as civic pillar)
he cheated: let on that he'd dropped

a coin or crust of bread, and bending, snuck
a final glimpse at Sodom. There's no gulling
God, though, so now as Lot's wife looked back
as well, God—fed up and recalling

that business in Eden—struck. He almost slew
Lot next, but Lot at least had feigned compliance;
looks count; Lot was the sort of pawn He could use.
And she? It wasn't so much her defiance

that got Him; gods hate a love they can't get inside.

TWO

THE WAKING

*Nor shall I care to write poetry that is
not praise, lamentation, or both.*
—Stamatis Smyrlis

EUROPA

a libretto

*Zeus and Queen Europa's court in Knossus, Crete, a few years
after her abduction, rape, and subsequent coronation. Her former
fiancé, Prince Hiram of Sidon, now an old man, appears on stage,
searching for Europa.*

HIRAM: Europa ...

EUROPA: I think I know him, but how can it be?
Just three summers gone
and he seems an old man.

HIRAM: Europa ... at last ...

EUROPA: The man I was to marry. Just three years, really?
How could time move so differently here?

HIRAM: Europa ... my wife.

EUROPA: No, I married another. I had no choice.

HIRAM: How long I searched—thirty years.

EUROPA: Speak softer, he's never far. Though your voice,
your voice—
it's sweet to hear. Your face has changed but not
your voice.

HIRAM: All the men who sailed with me, dead.

EUROPA: Still, leave and sail away while you can.
My husband the king is a god, not a man—
if you touch me, he'll kill you.

HIRAM: The god? You say a god?
Is that the way wives describe men in this place?
You should have stayed with me in Sidon.
I'd not have required such praise and ripe lies.

Some claimed they saw you leave,
but I could never believe
what they swore: that you left Sidon
on the back of a bull from the sea—
no natural thing, I agree,
and yet, no god.
What I can accept for a tale is this:
some foreign ship slipped in, with albino sails
like a bull's shining sides, and stole away
into the west,
bearing you.

I searched, as years passed,
from one nameless island to the next
until I was the last man, and at last
a rock crushed the hull off this coast
and I swam in to shore—
no god or beast to bear me.

But you look happy, and youthful still—
as if this place becomes you well—
as if for you no time has passed.
As if you miss nothing of your past.

EUROPA: The god gave a promise I'd never grow older.
Another gift, he told me,
and so it seemed at first.
Now it seems a curse.
I'd have stayed with you, believe me,
if the god had not deceived me—
but no, it's not so simple—listen—

HIRAM: So he is a god? And you love him?
You must. What good to have such power
if he can't force love—or lust—
to flower?

EUROPA: No—love, at least, is past such power.
That's why the gods hate and hurt us, my love.
Not able to die, they're unable to love—
and they long to know how it feels, more than power.

As for the tale, it is true.
It starts with a dream, my last night in Sidon:
two witches stand by my bed
and, in the way of dreams, nothing said,
I know they're bodies of land—continents.
The first is Asia, the other unnamed.
Asia says I'm hers, since I was born in Sidon.
From the other's reply I understand
Zeus will take me to some nameless land
and call it after me.

I woke unsettled. I summoned my friends,
asked them to come pick poppies in fields
by the sea—you know the place I mean,
where you and I have often gone.

There a bull appeared among our herds.
I never saw one so white, as if in robes,
so handsomely shaped,
smelling of the poppies he gently cropped,
lowing with the melodious sound
of a court musician on a wood flute.
The globes of his great brown eyes were tame.
I lost all fear. Over his horns I draped
flower-chains and stroked his hide.
At my feet he knelt, as if offering a ride
to a child. My friends were afraid,
but on I climbed. He leapt up and raced away
too fast for me to jump free. I cried for help,
to you, but now we were on the beach,
sand spattering behind us as the beast
charged into the shallows, swam on toward the west
at a speed beyond speed.

Here, on the beach, in the way of those
who can seize and keep what things they choose,
he made me, so he said, his queen.
Or, no, he gave me a choice—slave
in his cellars or queen in his bed.

HIRAM: You've suffered far worse than I.
You should have stayed with me in Sidon.
Maybe I too would still be young . . .

EUROPA: We'd both be old and both unfree—
I queen and you consort,
trapped in that tiny court,
flattered and lied to by courtiers.

HIRAM: And this is better? *Here* you're free?

EUROPA: I won't lie, not to one I've loved.
          Here too, courtiers, liars, intrigues, and the king
          who had a wife before me, others today,
          and others no doubt to come. And yet, and yet,
          that day and night on the spine of the god
          crossing between worlds . . . That passage
          over the night sea, with a dolphin entourage,
          far from land, outside of time,
          the god's sides aglow in dark water
          as if we soared not through seas but stars,
          made me forget life as a king's daughter,
          pampered, important, or so I'd believed.
          In that journey I was more alive than a god,
          than life itself. No court of sorrows
          would make me trade it—
          or so I've told myself, all these years—
          that those hours were my truest life,
          for which I lost you and all tomorrows.

HIRAM: And I my wife, and all tomorrows.

EUROPA: But didn't you gain something, for the loss?
          You lived in search of something precious,
          not mired and admired in idleness
          as I live now, forever, bearing
          gold-haired sons for a god
          who's forgotten me altogether,
          when I might have stayed with you
          in Sidon.

          [*She looks over her shoulder*]

You have to leave now.

HIRAM: Leave now? I've spent my whole life
           searching for an almost-wife
           and that life is spent.
           If this bull, god, king, or figment
           means to kill me, fine.
           I may be a fragment of what I was
           but can he do what I can do —
                                    die for you?
           That too is past his power, I think.
           With this touch —

EUROPA: No, please, for your sake. For mine.

HIRAM: If I die, I die.

EUROPA: If you do, so do I.

HIRAM: But you won't. You can't.

EUROPA: Not in your sense, no, but maybe in mine.

HIRAM: With this touch I marry and widow you at once.

EUROPA: I've been wrong.

HIRAM: To have stayed?

EUROPA: And to lie to myself for so long.
           Better to grieve than make peace through a lie.

HIRAM: Better I die, now I'm happy again.

EUROPA: Then touch me, take me back to Sidon.

HIRAM: A touch...takes us back to Sidon.

LATE COUPLET

Noli me tangere, *for Caesars I ame;*
And wylde for to hold, though I seme tame.
—Thomas Wyatt, c. 1535

Sometimes time turns perfect rhyme to slant
as in Wyatt's famous sonnet—how the couplet
no longer chimes, his *ame* turned *am,* now coupled
more by pattern, form. So everything gets bent
and slurred by time's shifts and edits. You and
I, for instance, no longer click or chord
the sharp way we did when suddenly paired
three decades back (not fifty—but human
prosody shifts faster),
                    and surely that's best—
half-rhyme is closer to human, and consonance,
not a flawless fit, is mostly what counts
over years. But still, this urge (from the past?
our blood?) to erase it all for one last run
at a unity: two worlds rhymed to one.

TO THE POET JEAN-BERNARD, NEAR ALDEBARAN

I said to her
whom you'd coveted so
for your own (forgive me, Jean,
forgive us), *Keep your eyes open
until you can't*—and on the very
dawn of your death we did try,
and failed, to maintain
that fusing gaze,
as you too that June morning
failed, lids lapsing—or did your eyes in fact
stay open, but at some point simply cease
to meet the day's unlidded light, to receive,
waferlike, a photon more of the world
you'd made love to
in *mots si justes*,
as you loved, no less
(in your wrong way)
her.
        Your body, Jean,
is laved now, levered slowly
down into *la fosse*,
that last, unlovered bed.
Jean, I am so sorry
for your loss,
our loss.

How a poet, impossible, must be
is—unenclosed wholly and yet

clamped shut—pores open
like portholes to the world

in welcome, yet unbreachable
as a safe, or carapace, case-

hardened against carious
words, spurious charms,

the germs of indigestible
trivia, by the gigabyte:

trite contagion. (Yet be curious
to the killing point.)

How must the poet flow?
Between these poles, impossibly,

and his goal, her goal—instantiate
in a phrase or stanza one moment

of flayed presence, in ways
no I-mind could counterfeit.

SPRINGTIDE

(Stéphane Mallarmé, 1862)

Sadly the morbid spring has chased away
winter, clear winter, season of serene art,
and desolate blood holds sway in my heart
where impotence, yawning, lolls and gapes.

Pale twilights turn tepid beneath my skull
bound like an old tomb with an iron torque,
and, rueful after dim, lovely dreams, I walk
over fields where floods of sap vaunt and spill.

Then, stricken by the trees' scents, I collapse,
so digging with my face a grave for my dreams,
and gnawing the warm earth where lilacs flaunt

I wait, sinking lower, for my ennui to mount . . .
though the Blue on the waking hedge now beams
and lifts into sunlit song flowering flocks.

Year by year the lindens he planted with his mother
tap deeper into the hills, root higher into the winds,
the slender limbs at midwinter stripped, the skies
Frisian blue. And on the lee slope a few hundred
spruce, once seedlings, now fill in
a solid, sun-annulling acre,
though they turn out to be balsam fir, not spruce,
her mistake and his, or maybe his alone —
in those days he assumed all evergreens
were "pines," or "spruce," whatever,
beyond his ego's stunted reach it was all whatever,
all lazy approximation. Now he believes little matters more
than knowing right names.

But the waking comes late.
In the early evening of a life, with dusk
redoubling in a still hectare of hemlock,
tamarack, redcone cedar, you might stir
out of self-induced coma and stare
years down into the mind —
                              too late, you might fear, this insight,
like others before it, might wane, the crucial life-change
fail to hold.
            Out of the spruce swale
he climbs a knoll into a third and final stand
they sowed a few weeks before she died,
during a brief and happy remission,
she looking years younger, quietly pleased
how the steroids had puffed her face enough
to fill in wrinkles, pad out the bones.

In ambering October light they dug
nursling birches into the knoll's bare scalp—
so now with every spring, it too seems
softened, freshened, aging in reverse,
while under the earth the roots of each
in fierce secrecy radiate like veins, fusing
further down into riches,
where all the mothers,
unfinished
unfolding,
remain.

In a sleeping pill season, in a REM-stage remission,
revisit a curve in a certain cold river

where the birches are in full business
and the grass of the banks is wild mint.

It's years, yet you're both stretched out here still,
rib to rib, hearts happily talking over each other,

and above you somehow the same southerlies,
same sunfish school of pewter leaves

pulsing in ultramarine. Remembrance:
how every touch and utterance

seemed tender calamity, so even now,
in the locked-in stasis of this sedation,

the couple you made is still current
on that earth. You were conscious, then,

even sleeping, and what's wholly lived keeps looping
through some unforgetting amnion, so pulse

to pulse, fully personed, you return. (Not that she can—
yet see how, even now, she is nowhere else.)

JUNE CANCELLATION

You make this small deposit to bank away, draw down
maybe years from now, in some sleeping pill season—
how the teens you're coaching, women,
almost, are all relegated to girlhood
by the storm.
              A synaptic charge
arcs the dusk—grand mal in the grey matter
of the clouds—and already the crash
cleaves you. Referee's whistle, first drops
spatting, and the girls are all fleeing,
cleats in hand, teams mixing
amid synchronous laughter,
none knowing now or caring
who won or lost,
                   as in the lost
novice seasons, years before this June
of mind-shears and limbic storms, self-
hunger, self-harm, many torrents far less
dodgeable than this storm,
and they will dodge this one,
and they know it,
                hence this riot
of evening reprieve, the school year almost served
and they shoeless on these rain-cool fields,
running—as if there is, while there is—home.

As she runs
through ice fog
with the white dog
in the hoarfrost
forest, the one
cardinal arc
colouring this
cold solstice
is the core
of her palpable heart.

build slowly, then linger. Think how the lone
sour note of some letdown, a little jab
or jilt, the kind that you'd work through soon

and forget, gets followed too closely
by the next, *We regret to inform you* (by email
or post), or some other fleeting, non-fatal snub—

then the clincher, the sharp or flat
that nails the chord, a lauded colleague's cocktail
froideur, or just a driver at a four-way

giving you the finger. So now again the minor
fall: you drag through days in a somber key,
like aftertones of a verdict murmured, you to you,

in the night. *Hey, loser.* Every failure
seems a small demise, a strange homecoming;
knowing it's not never helps. Brain gets wiser, gut

never gets it, stays a sucker too for the dulcet
jingles of praise, lucky runs, ribbons, raises,
as if fifty years of learning meant squat,

win or lose, captain or cut from the squad,
the limbic centre sends up its flares.
How come you weren't at the big bash?

How you would like to transcend this primate
sadnesss (*what bash?*) we try to understand
and salve with poems, paintings, songs or prayer—

solo protests against solitude—a repertoire
reeling you back beyond years to that amnio
cosmos before chords, major, minor,

diminished: just a slow, enveloping tempo
without tune, before mother
casts you out to face the band.

As the speaker sensed he was nearing time—
his "twelve to fifteen minutes" lapsing
by the second, the syllable, too little left
to finish—he sped up, tightening the white
space between words like a printer's devil,
squeezing the kerning, shrinking, so to speak,
the font, then hurdling clauses, scrapping pauses,
skipping or tongue-torquing words—honestly
trying to make time!—until, flicking eyes to the clock,
he saw the minute-hand lopping off
his last seconds, though so few words remained
(a mere paragraph—three at most), and so
he drew a determined breath
and slowed into them.
                He strove not to note the bulleted eyes
of the MC flapping her flashcard, FIFTEEN
MINUTES!—a skinflint quantum, it struck him now,
script done,
           so setting it down he went live, went *rogue*,
footlighting what he'd said so far, igniting
each thought off the last
like a chainsmoker of concepts—ignoring
the delegates' writhing and the MC's
frenzied flashcard, his mouth motile
as a set of joke-shop teeth
or the mandibles of Pound
with his cantos beyond counting,
                  NO MADAM,
I WILL NOT, he filibustered on and left no gap
where one might interject or even clap

and so mute him, in the way that time,
he saw now, was bound to,
                            death,
he knew now, is the deafest
of many indifferent locales,
a kind of green-room sealed, no curtain-
call coming, and what is silence now
but a redundant rehearsal
for that lonely coda?

So on he talked, castigating the clock-face
on behalf of every bore who ever prattled
and the full race of the forlorn and rarely heeded,
in his heat, his fury—his audience
fading now, thinning out, *mine enemy*
LISTEN TO ME only
LISTEN
for once in your
for once in my
a few minutes of
god damn it people
is it too much to

ICE, EDEN

(Paul Celan, German translator of Emily Dickinson)

There is a country—lost—
A moon swells in its reeds—
And something gnawed by frost
(Like us) there glows and sees—

Sees, since it has eyes—
Each eye an earth, aglint—
The night, the night, the lyes—
*Es sieht, das Augenkind.**

It sees, it sees—we see—
Before this hour is done
I see you, and you too see—
The ice will rise, like bone—

* "It sees, this eye-child"

73

Diving beyond the light, the swimmer
carries the sun down with her
as a dimming nimbus of heat on skin

or trapped under the cap with her hair;
as sun-warmed air in the soft tanks of her lungs;
a thermal reserve in that minor star

of moody hydrogen, her heart.
As if she might colonize and humanize
these depths any more than deep space;

as if this time, despite quantum odds,
after how many dives, she might be able to stay—
evolve in one lunge, like the ancestral

monster portrayed in musty bio texts:
bold, panting pioneer who flippers up
onto land; proto-mammal who returns to the waves,

switching elements as simply as changing address.
And at times, in dreams, you do the same—
find yourself flying, atoned in the upper air,

or a gilled thing plying a placental abyss
beyond gravity, grave, or ego—the full sorrow
of self-knowing—at least until waking, when,

yet again, you birth yourself back up onto shore.

YONAOSHI

Inochi no umi, shi no umi

In less than two weeks the disaster
will hemorrhage out of the headlines
onto page whatever,
its span done faster than the brief
half-life of iodine—but for now,
with a dozen aftershocks still to Richter,
an old woman stands alone
in a flooded field of debris, no human
screen to frame her, chanting
yonaoshi, yonaoshi:
May the world be restored.

Sea of life, sea

of death——*my soul seeks out a mountain*
that can stand in this surge.

VARIATIONS ON LINES HEARD IN A DREAM

1

The reading of the will:
final cricket bequeathing
all she owns in the world,
her call.

2

Last cricket's fading summation
fails to sway
the mute, faceless jury.
Summer's sad attorney.

3

Final cricket's
last credo in the fields —
the voice dies still believing.

AUTHOR'S NOTE

My last two poetry collections, *The Address Book* and *Patient Frame*, both end with a section of "approximations"—free translations of poems by various authors modern and ancient, renowned and obscure. In this new book, I've opted not to sequester the translations but instead to integrate them with my own poems. This approach involves a certain optical risk; I might seem to be proposing an equality between new lines of my own and (for example) classic cadences by Anna Akhmatova. But this integrated design really just reflects how every piece here, original or translated, emerges from a single period and process of reading and pondering, writing and revising. I work on approximations concurrently with my own poems, so the two forms are always in dialogue on my desk—my engagement with a poem by Georg Trakl, say, inspiring a poem of my own, which in turn, as it develops, suggests new ways to improve or complicate the Trakl translation. So it's in hope of creating a more coherent, dynamic, and naturally flowing book that I've interleaved original and approximated work.

I'd like to acknowledge here, gratefully, that George McWhirter first suggested I use the term "approximation."

S.H., Kingston, September, 2015

NOTES ON POEMS & APPROXIMATIONS

"The City" is one of the best-known poems of Cavafy (Konstantínos Kaváfis), and a number of literally accurate English translations exist. But even the best of these, by Edmund Keeley and Philip Sherrard, is more a rendering in prose—albeit fluent, elegant prose—than a poetic translation. In my opinion, a translator should try to represent not only the content of the original but also its form and sound, especially if the poem has a rhyme scheme, as does "The City."

Since "The City" is written in such straightforward, transparent Greek, there can be little argument among translators about how to render particular word-choices or metaphorical constructions. Hence readers will find little difference between the various unrhymed English versions of the poem. What most of these versions do convey well is the stately, processional movement of Cavafy's thoughts and words—and without question this movement is a key part of Cavafy's poetic signature. But in "The City" the other vital component is rhyme.

Of course, translators who do attempt to re-enact the verbal music of a rhyming poem may fail in their own ways. In trying to approximate the effect of Cavafy's end-rhymed Greek, I've used consonantal—and, in one or two cases, assonantal—rhyme, for the usual reason: English is a relatively rhyme-poor tongue, and the consonantal system evens the field for English-language translators, allowing them to achieve the effect of rhyme without overly distorting and deforming the poem's movement. (A liberal use of internal rhyme, I feel, helps support and deepen the effect.)

"Song of the Graves" (*Canción de las sepulturas*): J. E. Villalta, thought by some to have been a sort of escaped and renegade heteronym of Fernando Pessoa, was actually a Spanish poet who published only one book, *Canciones y otras canciones*, and who, while continuing to write in Spanish, lived in Rio Tinto, Portugal, for most of his life (1907–88).

"The Weather Online" is a kind of approximation of Lucinda Williams's beautiful song "I Envy the Wind" (from her 2001 album, *Essence*). Williams's song is itself a kind of approximation of Emily Dickinson's poem 498, "I envy Seas, whereon He rides."

"Lot's Wife" and "Lot Looked Back First": While Lot's wife is not named in the Bible, other sources give her name as either Ado or Edith.

The libretto "Europa" was commissioned by Larry Beckwith, artistic director of the Toronto Masque Theatre. James Rolfe composed the score. The short opera premiered, as *Europa and the White Bull*, on April 25, 2014, at Trinity-St. Paul's Centre, Toronto. My thanks also to managing director Vivian Moens.

The libretto is dedicated to the memory of poet Symon Beckwith (1956–2003).

"Evolutions" is after a fibre artwork, *Swimming in the Deep End*, by Kingston artist Mary Ev Wyatt.

"*Yonaoshi*": the italicized epigraph means "Sea of life, sea of death." The italicized final stanza is an approximation of an old, anonymous Japanese poem.

ACKNOWLEDGEMENTS

Versions of some of the poems in this book were first published in the magazines, digital sites, and anthologies listed below. The author is very grateful to the editors.

London Review of Books
Best American Poetry (2012: edited by Mark Doty)
TLR
Eighteen Bridges
The Walrus
The Malahat Review
The New Quarterly
Canadian Literature
Dusie
Scrivener
PRISM international
The Best of Walrus Poetry (edited by Michael Lista)

I also want to thank by name the people who commented on one or a number of the poems as they evolved: Mary Huggard, Michael Holmes, Sandra Ridley, Jenny Haysom, Shane Neilson, Ginger Pharand, Christine Wiesenthal, Paul Kelley, and Alexander Scala.

I was very lucky to have Damian Rogers as my editor for the full collection. She helped reorganize the book in several important respects and I really can't thank her enough.

Peter Norman's copy-edit was thorough, astute, sympathetic, and mostly painless.

Over the last several years I've been fortunate to serve as a writer-in-residence at McGill University (the Mordecai Richler Residency) and at Queen's University in Kingston. My thanks to the residency organizers, Allan Hepburn at McGill and Carolyn Smart at Queen's, and to the institutions themselves. Finally, a thank you to the Ontario Arts Council for its support of these poems.

S.H.

Steven Heighton's poetry collections include *Stalin's Carnival*, which won the Gerald Lampert Memorial Award in 1990 and appeared in a new edition in 2013; *The Ecstasy of Skeptics*, a Governor General's Award finalist; *The Address Book*, poems from which received the Petra Kenney Prize and a gold National Magazine Award; and *Patient Frame*, poems from which received the P.K. Page Award and a silver National Magazine Award. Heighton is also the author of several acclaimed works of fiction, including the Trillium Award finalists *Flight Paths of the Emperor* and *The Dead Are More Visible* and the novel *Afterlands*, which was a *New York Times Book Review* Editors' Choice and was cited on best-of-year lists in ten publications in Canada, the U.S., and the U.K. His poems and stories have appeared in *London Review of Books*, *Poetry*, *Tin House*, *Zoetrope: All-Story*, *Brick*, *Best American Poetry*, *The Walrus*, *Europe*, *TLR*, *AGNI*, *Poetry London*, *New England Review*, *Best Canadian Poetry* and *Best English Stories*. He lives in Kingston, Ontario.